1 A tour of the Universe

What is a planet?
▼ A **planet** is a body which **orbits** (travels around) a star. The planet **Earth** orbits the Sun (our nearest star).

What is a moon?
▼ A **moon** is a body w travels around the Earth. Most of the other planets have moons.

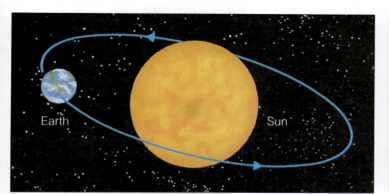

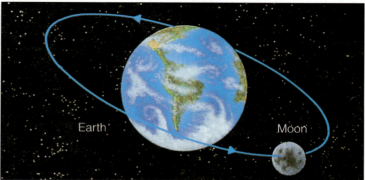

What is the Solar System?
▶ The Solar System is the Sun and all the bodies **orbiting** it: the nine planets, their moons, the asteroids and their comets.

What is a star?
▶ A star is a huge ball of hot glowing gas. A star produces its own heat and light by nuclear reactions. The Sun is a star.

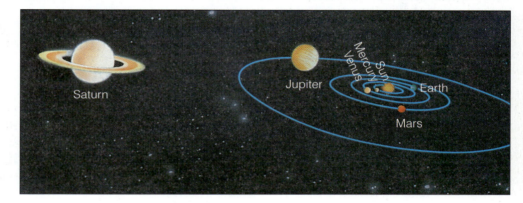

What is a galaxy?
▼ A galaxy is a huge group of stars held together by gravity. Earth is part of the **Milky Way** galaxy.

What is the Universe?
▼ The Universe contains one hundred thousand million galaxies. It contains everything that exists.

Q1 Draw a picture to show how the Earth moves around the Sun.

Q2 Put the Moon, Sun and Earth in order of size, starting with the largest.

Q3 List the four planets nearest the Sun.

Q4 List three other bodies which are found in the Solar System.

Extension sheet 1 can be used now.

2 The Earth

How the Earth moves

In this activity you will see that the Earth spins on its **axis** as it travels around the Sun. It takes 24 hours to make one full spin but it takes a year to travel around the Sun.

Apparatus
☐ torch

A Work with a partner. The person acting as the *Sun* holds the torch and the person acting as the *Earth* stands two metres away in the light of the torch. ▼

B Earth turns **anticlockwise** (to the left) to show how it spins on its axis. In real time it takes the Earth 24 hours to make one complete turn. ▼

C To show how the Earth moves round the Sun, *Earth* walks in an anticlockwise circle round the *Sun* but keeps turning anticlockwise as well. The *Sun* turns the torch slowly as the *Earth* moves round. ▼

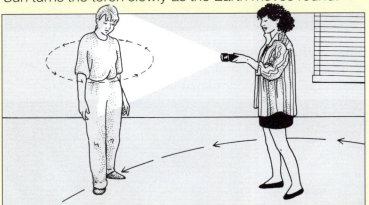

D Complete one full turn around the *Sun*. In real time this would take **one year**, which is about 365 days. Swap positions with your partner and repeat **A**, **B** and **C**. ▼

A leap year has 366 days in it

If we are very exact about the length of one year then we would say it is 365 days, 5 hours and 46 seconds. If we take the hours, minutes and seconds and multiply by four we get 23 hours, 15 minutes and 4 seconds. (This is almost one day.) Every fourth year the month of February has 29 days in it, instead of 28. Every fourth year is called a **leap year**.

Q1 Copy the diagram.

Q2 Put two arrows on your diagram to show how the Earth moves.

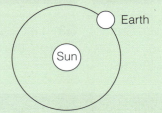

Q3 How many full turns does the Earth make about its own **axis**, when it travels once round the Sun?

Q4 How long does it take the Earth to travel half-way round the Sun?

Q5 Which of the following years are leap years: 1988, 1990, 1994, 1996?

2 The Earth

Day and night

Let us find out why we have day and night. Our day is 24 hours long.

Apparatus
- ☐ globe of the Earth
- ☐ torch ☐ Plasticine
- ☐ thin card ☐ sticky tape
- ☐ clamp and stand

A Make a small figure out of Plasticine and place it on Britain. ▼

B In a darkened classroom shine the torch light on the figure as shown. When the figure is in the light it is day time. ▼

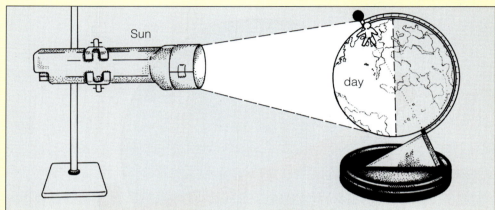

C Spin the globe slowly through half a turn anticlockwise. When the figure is in the dark it is night time. ▼

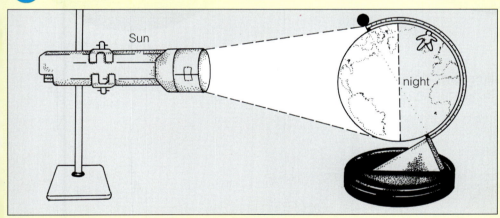

Day and night at the poles

▼ The **poles** have six months of days followed by six months of nights. When the North Pole is in the dark the South Pole is in the light. This is because the Earth is spinning on a tilt.

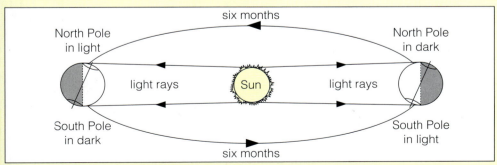

Q1 If you were at these positions, would it be day or night?

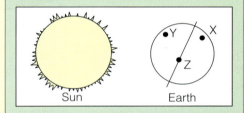

Q2 Why can only half of the Earth be in daylight at any one time?

Q3 Copy the diagram below:
a shade the *night* side
b label the *day* side
c draw and label the poles
d which pole is in the dark?

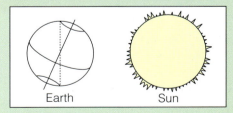

Q4 Explain why the poles have six months of light followed by six months of darkness.

Extension exercise 2 can be used now.

2 The Earth

The Earth's tilt
▼ The imaginary line which the Earth spins about is called the Earth's **axis of rotation**. This is tilted by 23.5 degrees to the vertical. It is the tilt which causes the seasons. In Britain the North Pole is tilted towards the Sun in summer and away from the Sun in winter.

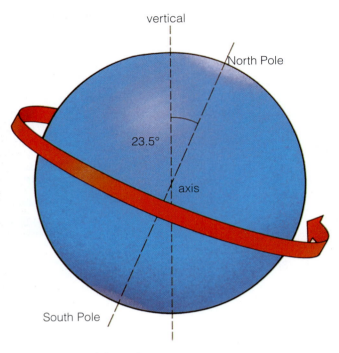

The equator
▼ The Earth is divided into two by another imaginary line called the **equator**. The part above the equator is called the **northern hemisphere**. The part below the equator is called the **southern hemisphere**. Europe is in the northern hemisphere, Australia is in the southern hemisphere.

The direction of the Earth's axis
▼ The north pole always points in the same direction (towards the **Pole Star**) no matter where the Earth is in its journey around the Sun.

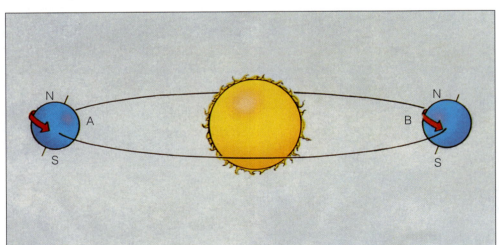

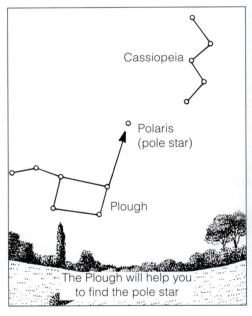

The Plough will help you to find the pole star

Q1 Draw and label the Earth with the following: axis, equator, poles and hemispheres.

Q2 Which pole is at the top of the northern hemisphere?

Q3 This pole always points to a star. Name the star.

Q4 The Earth's tilt causes some changes. What are they?

Q5 In the diagram on the left what season is it at A and (then) at B in the northen hemisphere?

2 The Earth

Sun's rays on the Earth

In this activity we shall find out why the number of daylight hours and the solar energy we receive change throughout the year.

Apparatus
☐ clamp and stand
☐ torch ☐ globe

A Set up the apparatus as in the picture. The northern hemisphere is tilted away from the Sun. This is winter in Britain. ▼

B Change the globe's position, as shown. The northern hemisphere is now tilted towards the Sun. This is summer in Britain. ▼

Paths of the Sun across the sky

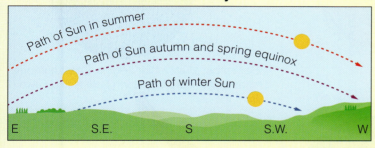

Two effects which cause our summer

The path of the Sun in summer shows that it is higher in the sky and its **arc** across the sky is longer. Daytime is longer which means there is more time for heating the Earth's surface. ◀

The Sun's rays are also more **perpendicular** (directly above us) than in the winter which results in a higher **concentration** of solar energy per square metre. ▼

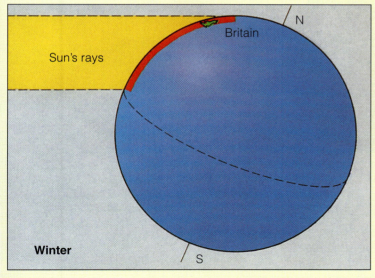
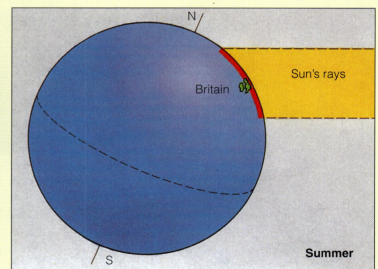

Q1 In **A** which hemisphere receives the most sunlight?

Q2 In **B** which pole is in total darkness and in which hemisphere is it winter?

Q3 Write down two effects which cause our winter.

Q4 Do you expect seasonal changes at the equator to be small or large? Explain your answer.

5

2 The Earth

The four seasons

As the Earth travels around the Sun we experience different climate changes. The picture shows the Earth at the start of each season in the northern hemisphere.

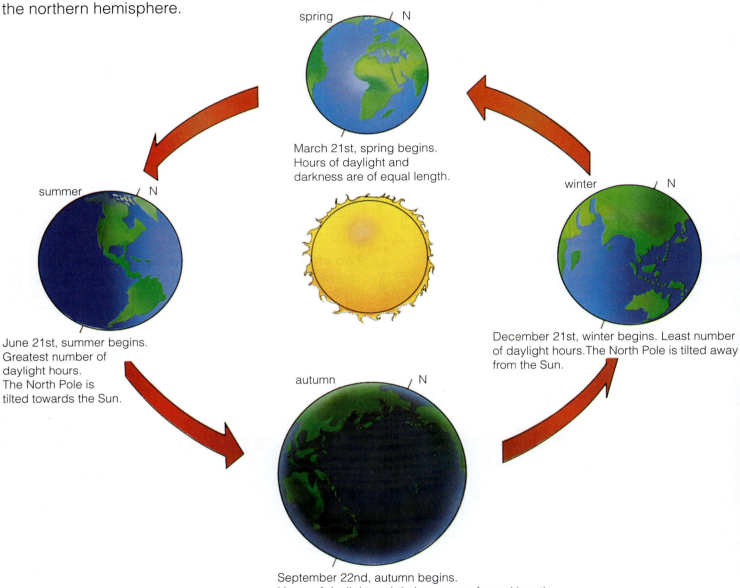

spring / N
March 21st, spring begins. Hours of daylight and darkness are of equal length.

summer / N
June 21st, summer begins. Greatest number of daylight hours. The North Pole is tilted towards the Sun.

winter / N
December 21st, winter begins. Least number of daylight hours. The North Pole is tilted away from the Sun.

autumn / N
September 22nd, autumn begins. Hours of daylight and darkness are of equal length.

Q1 Write down the starting dates for each of the seasons.

Q2 Write down the season and the date of the day with the greatest number of daylight hours.

Q3 Write down the season and the date of the day with the least number of daylight hours.

Q4 What happens to the hours of daylight between
a autumn and winter
b winter and spring
c spring and summer
d summer and autumn?

Q5 What season is it in the southern hemisphere when the North Pole is pointing away from the Sun?

Extension exercise 3 can be used now.

3 Gravity

What on earth is gravity?

Gravity is the **force of attraction** between all pieces of **matter**.

▼ All things, large and small have gravity, but to feel the gravitational pull of something, it has to have a very large mass, for example like the Earth.

▼ Larger planets have a stronger pull of gravity than smaller planets.

▼ The force of gravity gets smaller as you move away from the Earth.

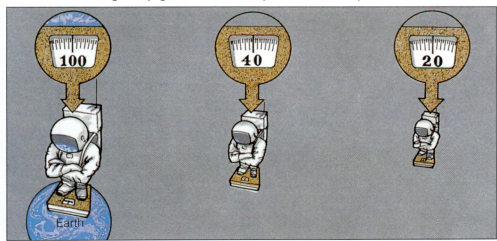

Since the day you were born you have been feeling the pull of the Earth's gravity on you. It's called your **weight**. Weight is another name for the force of attraction between your **mass** and the mass of the Earth. As you grow your mass gets bigger, so the force of attraction between you and the Earth gets bigger and this is why your weight gets bigger.

You have learnt that the Earth is shaped like a ball – it is gravity which stops us falling off it. It is the Sun's gravity which holds the planets in their **elliptical** paths around it. Gravity holds the Universe and all the things in it together.

Q1 What is gravity?

Q2 Why are astronauts lighter on the Moon than on the Earth, even though they have the same *mass*?

Q3 Jupiter's mass is almost 320 times the mass of the Earth. Which of these two planets has the larger pull of gravity?

Q4 Where would you have the greater *weight,* on Jupiter or on the Earth?

Q5 The diagram below shows four bottles placed on the Earth's surface. Copy the diagram and draw what happens when a small amount of water is poured into each bottle.

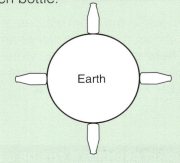

3 Gravity

Measuring your mass and weight

In this experiment you are going to measure your mass in kilograms and convert it into your weight in newtons.

Apparatus
☐ bathroom scales ☐ calculator

Q1 Copy this table.

My mass (kg)	My weight (N)

weight = mass × gravitational field strength
(N)   (kg)   (N/kg)

A Stand on the scales and record your mass in kilograms in the table. This is the amount of matter which you are made from. If you do not want to weigh yourself, pretend you are 60 kg. ▶

B Your weight depends on your mass and the pull of the planet you are standing on. Earth pulls down every kilogram at its surface with a force of 10 newtons (N). We say it has a **gravitational field strength** of 10 N per kg. Use the equation to work out your weight and put it in the table. ▲

Q2 Copy this table.

Name of planet	Gravitational field strength (N/kg)	My mass on the planet (kg)	My weight on the planet (N)
Mars	3.8		

Mars 3.8 N/kg

Saturn 11.9 N/kg

Jupiter 26.9 N/kg

Neptune 12.2 N/kg

C Look at the four pictures above. Each one shows a different planet and its **gravitational field strength**. If you were standing on the surface of each planet calculate what your weight would be. Fill in the table. ▲

Q3 Where are you the lightest?

Q4 Where are you the heaviest?

Q5 Which measurement stays the same no matter which planet you are on?

Extension exercise 4 can be used now.

4 Satellites

Apparatus

☐ rubber bung tied to string

 Stand clear of others when you swing the bung.

The word **satellite** is used to describe any object which moves around another. The Moon is a **natural** satellite of the Earth. In 1957, Russia launched **Sputnik 1**, the first **artificial** satellite. It was about the size of a football. About 5000 satellites circle the Earth today. They use **solar panels** to change the Sun's rays into electricity for all their electrical power needs. They do not need to be streamlined (like rockets) because far above the Earth there is no air to be pushed through.

Satellites are kept in orbit by the pull of the Earth's gravity. This **gravitational** force always acts towards the centre of the Earth pulling the satellite around in a circular orbit.

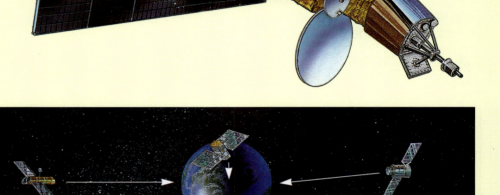
gravitational force towards Earth's centre

A Carefully swing the bung above your head as in the picture. This is a model of how a satellite moves around the Earth. ▼

Q1 What is a satellite?

Q2 Which energy source do satellites use?

Q3 What energy change takes place in solar panels?

Q4 What force keeps a satellite in orbit?

Q5 Copy the diagram. It shows the same satellite in different positions in orbit. Draw the force arrows on the satellite in the positions shown.

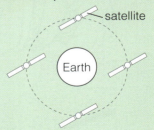

Q6 What do you notice about the direction of the force as the satellite moves?

4 Satellites

Making a model of a geosynchronous satellite

Apparatus
- satellite cutout ☐ scissors
- drawing pin ☐ cork mat
- calculator ☐ pen

Geosynchronous satellites travel around the Earth once every 24 hours. They orbit the equator at a height of 36 000 km and a speed of 3 km/s. From the Earth they look as though they are not moving. They appear to be stationary above a point on the Earth's surface. With only three geosynchronous satellites in orbit we can send and receive messages from anywhere on Earth. These messages can be sent very quickly because radio waves travel at the speed of light. Geosynchronous satellites are moving very fast. In this activity you are going to make a model to help us to see why they appear as though they are not moving when we look at them from Earth.

A Cut out the discs on the satellite cutout. Place the centre of disc A on top of the centre of disc B. Connect them with the drawing pin on a cork mat. ▼

B Line up the dish aerial on the Earth with the geosynchronous satellite as shown. ▼

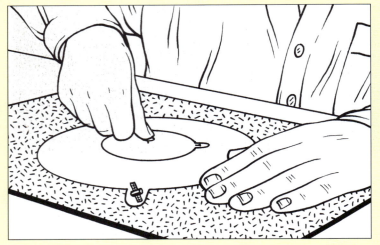

C You rotate the dish aerial while your friend moves the satellite so that it keeps up with the dish aerial. Stop at the same time. The satellite should still be above the dish aerial. To a person standing on Earth it looks as if the satellite has not moved. ▶

Q1 How many degrees must the satellite move through to keep up with the dish aerial as it moves through 90 degrees?

Q2 What do you notice about the distance moved by a geosynchronous satellite compared to the distance moved by the dish aerial?

Q3 Explain why the geosynchronous satellite must have a greater speed than the dish aerial.

Extension exercise 5 can be used now.

4 Satellites

Communicating with satellites

Special stations are built on Earth to communicate with satellites. They use dish **aerials** to send and receive **radio waves** to and from satellites. To stop the signals from getting mixed up satellites send signals and receive signals using different **frequencies** of radio waves.

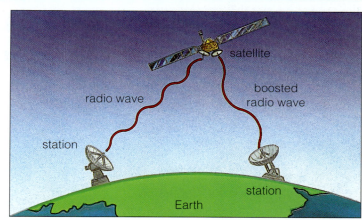

Uses of satellites

What are satellites useful for?
- telephone conversations
- space exploration
- weather forecasting
- military 'spy' satellites
- oil and gas exploration
- television programmes
- navigation
- charting maps
- scientific research in weightless conditions
- radio programmes

Sea satellites
▼ These are used to link signals from ships and oil rigs to the normal telephone network.

Landsat
▲ These help us to find gas and oil, keep track of pollution and give drought and famine warnings. Diseased crops show up blue-black and healthy crops in pink and red.

Television satellites
◀ The television company, BSkyB, send television programmes into our homes via satellites. A satellite dish aerial can be fixed to your house so that you can receive these programmes.

Q1 List six uses of satellites.

Q2 Imagine you were making a phone call to Australia via satellite links. Draw a picture to show the path of your communication.

5 The Moon

How the Earth, Moon and Sun move

In this activity we shall make a model to show how the Earth, Moon and Sun move. The time interval from one new Moon to the next new Moon is 29.5 days.

Apparatus
- ☐ scissors ☐ 3 paper fasteners
- ☐ Sun-Moon-Earth cutout
- ☐ large sheet of sugar paper

A Cut round the circles on your sheet. Colour the *Sun* yellow, the *Earth* green and the *Moon* red. Use a paper fastener to join the two dots labelled S together. ▶

B Join together the three dots labelled E. Join the two dots labelled M together as in the picture. ▼

C You can show the movement of the Moon, Earth and Sun by turning the circles *anticlockwise*. ▼

The **plane** of the Moon's orbit makes an angle of around 5° with the **plane of the** Earth's orbit. Your model does not show this. ▼

Moon's orbit round the Earth — Sun — Earth's orbit round the Sun

Q1 Put arrows on your model to show how the Earth, Moon and Sun move.

Q2 Move the Earth through one turn. How long does it take the Earth to make one orbit of the Sun?

Q3 Move the Moon's disc through one turn. How long does it take the Moon to make one orbit of the Earth?

Q4 Start with the model you have made in the position below. Draw a diagram to show their position:
a 14 days later
b 6 months later.

Q5 Extend your model to include the planet Mars.

5 The Moon

The Moon – the facts

▼ The Moon is the Earth's natural satellite. The gravitational force between the Earth and the Moon keep it in orbit. The Moon does not produce its own light, it **reflects** the light of the Sun. This is why it looks so bright in the night sky.

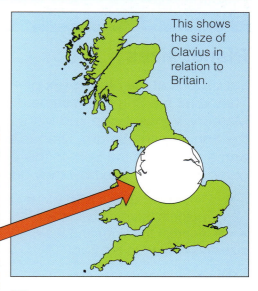

This shows the size of Clavius in relation to Britain.

There are over 500 000 craters on the Moon. They are caused by meteorites (large rocks) crashing onto its surface. One of the larger ones is called Clavius.

▼ The Moon's gravitational field strength is one sixth that of the Earth. For this reason things fall much more slowly on the Moon than on Earth.

▼ It would take 81 Moons to equal the mass of the Earth.

1 Earth   81 Moons

Apollo 17 (launched 7/11/72) Eugene Cernan and Harrison Schmitt landed on the edge of the Sea of Serenity on 11/11/72.

▶ There is no air on the Moon – it has no atmosphere, so there are no storms and no rain. Footprints left behind by astronauts will remain for millions of years. You cannot hear any sound because air is needed to carry sound from place to place.

Because there is no atmosphere to absorb the Sun's rays the daytime temperature on the Moon can be as high as 130°C. At night the temperature can be as low as −153°C because there is no atmosphere to slow down heat loss from the Moon's soil.

Q1 What force keeps the Moon in its orbit?

Q2 Why does the Moon look so bright at night if it does not produce any light?

Q3 What would you weigh on the Moon? Gravitational field strength of Moon = 1.6 N/kg.

Q4 The Moon has no atmosphere. Explain **a** why this causes large temperature differences between night and day and **b** why there are many craters on the Moon.

Extension exercise 6 can be used now.

6 The planets

Planet sizes

Let us look at the other eight planets which travel around the Sun. They orbit the Sun in the same direction in almost circular paths. Mercury, Venus, Earth and Mars have small diameters and are near the Sun. Jupiter, Saturn, Uranus and Neptune have large diameters and are far from the Sun. In this activity let us make a scale model of the planets to see how they compare with the size of the Earth. ▼

Apparatus

☐ card ☐ ruler ☐ scissors
☐ drawing compasses
☐ Sun model

A The table shows a list of the planets (starting with the one nearest the Sun) and their sizes compared to the Earth. ▼

Planet	Relative size (cm)
Mercury	0.4
Venus	0.9
Earth	1.0
Mars	0.5
Jupiter	11.0
Saturn	9.4
Uranus	4.0
Neptune	3.8
Pluto	0.2

B Using the measurements in the table draw nine circles, one for each planet. Label each circle with the planet's name. Cut them out and put them in the same order as they are in the table. Put the Sun model next to Mercury. Compare the planet sizes. ▼

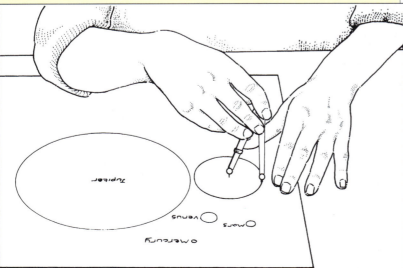

Q1 Copy this table.

Bigger than Earth (starting with the biggest)	Smaller than Earth (starting with the smallest)

Q2 Complete the table with the names of the planets.

Q3 How many known planets are there in the Solar System?

Q4 List the names of **a** the inner planets **b** the outer planets

Q5 Make up a **mnemonic** to help you to remember the names and positions of the planets. **ROY G**oes **B**oating **I**n **V**enice is a mnemonic to help you to remember the order of colours of light in the visible spectrum.

6 The planets

How far away are the planets?

The distances between the planets are huge. Most of the Solar System is empty space. It takes light 5.5 hours to reach us from Pluto. The five **outer planets** are cold and dark because they are great distances from the Sun. The four **inner planets** are much hotter because they are nearer the Sun and receive a lot of its energy.

The next activity compares how far away the planets are from the Sun.

Apparatus
- scale models of planets
- model of the Sun
- measuring tape
- calculator

A Work in a group of ten. Choose a planet. This is the *planet* you are going to be in the activity. The table shows the average distances of the planets from the Sun. ▼

Planet	Average distance from Sun (million km)
Mercury	58
Venus	108
Earth	150
Mars	228
Jupiter	778
Saturn	1 427
Uranus	2 870
Neptune	4 497
Pluto	5 900

B Use a scale of 1 cm = **1 Mkm**. (1 Mkm = 1 000 000 km). Make a table with the names of the people in your group, the planet they are going to be and the distance they must stand from the Sun in centimetres. ▼

C Ask your teacher if you can carry out **B** outside or in a long corridor. The *Sun* should not move once the measurement begins. Measure your distance from the *Sun* and stay there until everyone has got into position. From your position look at the *Sun* and then at the other planets. Notice the scale of the distances. ▼

Q1 Why is it warmer on the inner planets than the outer ones?

Q2 What is the average distance of Mercury from the Sun?

Q3 What is the average distance of Mars from Earth?

Q4 On average how many km is Neptune from Earth?

Q5 Describe what the Sun would look like from Pluto.

Q6 Explain why it is colder and darker on the outer planets.

The planets

What's it like on the other planets?

Earth is the only planet known to support life. This is because it has water and oxygen and other things which support life. If it were closer to the Sun it would have been too hot for life to develop. If we were further away it would have been too cold. It was a delicate balance of **elements**, position and **temperature** which let living systems develop on Earth and not on the other planets.

Q1 Make the planets cutout.

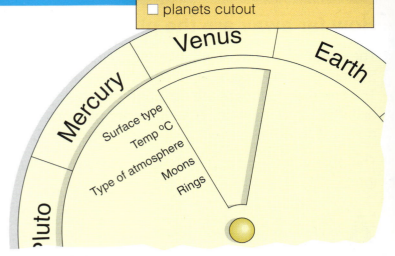

Apparatus

☐ planets cutout

Mercury
◀ Mercury has no atmosphere. It is rocky and covered in craters. The surface temperature is −173°C to 427°C. It has no moons or rings. It has no life.

Venus
▼ Venus is covered with rocky craters and volcanic mountains. It has a thick atmosphere of **sulphuric acid** and **carbon dioxide** which stops heat loss. Its surface temperature is 457°C. It has no moons. It has no life.

Jupiter
▶ Jupiter has an atmosphere of **hydrogen**, **helium**, **ammonia** and **methane**. Its surface is all gas. Its surface temperature is −108°C. It has 16 moons and one ring. There is no life on Jupiter.

▼ The **Red Spot** is a huge storm cloud. It is three times bigger than our Earth.

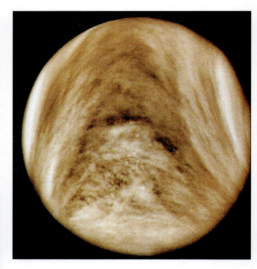

Q2 Use the pictures and information to complete the cutout.

6 The planets

Saturn
▼ The surface is all gas – hydrogen, helium, ammonia and methane. Its surface temperature is –139°C. It has at least 18 moons and many rings, but no life.

Mars
▼ It is rocky with lots of craters and volcanoes. Its surface temperature ranges from –143°C to 17°C. The atmosphere is carbon dioxide. It has two moons and no life.

Neptune
▼ Its surface temperature is –199°C. It has 8 moons. Its surface is covered in gas made up of hydrogen, helium and methane. It has no life.

Saturn's rings
▼ The rings are made up of tiny rocky particles frozen in ice.

Pluto
▼ The surface is rocky. It is covered in solid frozen water and methane. Its surface temperature is –233°C. It has one moon and no rings. It has no life.

Charon (Pluto's moon)

Pluto

Uranus
▼ The surface is all gas – hydrogen, helium, ammonia and methane. It has 15 moons and 11 rings. Its surface temperature is –197°C. It has no life.

Q3 Name the planets which have more than two moons.

Q4 Why do you think these planets have so many moons?

Q5 Which planets have no moons?

Q6 Why do you think these planets have no moons?

Q7 Why do you think Venus is hotter than Mercury even though Mercury is nearer the Sun?

Q8 Why do you think Pluto is frozen solid?

Q9 Explain why you think life developed on Earth and not on the other planets.

Extension exercise 7 can be used now.

7 Comets

Apparatus
☐ comet cutout ☐ scissors
☐ glue

Orbits of comets
▶ **Comets** move around the Sun in either **elliptical** or **hyperbolic** orbits. A comet with a hyperbolic orbit escapes from the Solar System. It is never seen again. We can predict where and when to expect comets with elliptical orbits.

▶ **Halley's** comet has an elliptical orbit. It is the most famous of all comets. It takes 76 years to complete a full orbit and it last returned in March 1986. Records show that it has been observed for over 2 200 years.

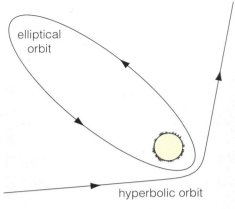

Structure of comets
■ Comets have a solid **nucleus** (middle) which is like a 'dirty snowball' of ice and dust particles. Around the nucleus is a **coma** (head). It too is made up of gas and dust.
■ As it gets nearer the Sun the comet gets hotter. The dirty ice begins to evaporate making a gigantic tail of **charged particles** of gas and dust particles.
■ When light falls on the dust particles it is reflected and this is why we can see this part of the tail.

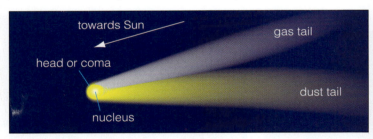

■ The **solar wind** (which is also made up of charged particles given out by the Sun), along with the Sun's radiation, exerts a force on the comet's tail, pushing it away from the Sun. For this reason when a comet is moving away from the Sun it actually travels tail first.

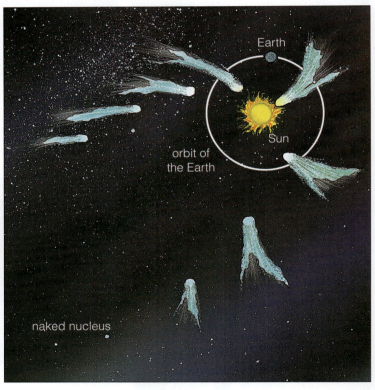

Comets 'wear out' eventually
As a comet returns again and again to the neighbourhood of the Sun it loses more and more gas and dust. Eventually the dust and gas are completely 'boiled away' and the comet can no longer be seen in the night sky. Comets have a **lifespan** of about 10 million years which is short compared to the age of the Solar System (4.6 billion years). The comets that we see today probably started to come near the Sun only recently. Scientists think that a large cloud of comets exist beyond Pluto. **Gravitational changes** in the cloud cause new comets to be pulled in towards the Solar System replacing those that have 'worn out'.

Q1 What is the nucleus of a comet made from?

Q2 Comets do not give out light. How can we see them?

Q3 Why does a comet's tail point away from the Sun?

Q4 When will Halley's comet return next?

Q5 How many times has Halley's comet made a complete orbit of the Sun? (Assume its first visit was 2200 years ago.)

Q6 Why do you think the brightness of a comet gets less as it gets older?

8 Stars

The Sun is our nearest star

Apparatus
- ☐ video camera ☐ blank tape
- ☐ TV and video player
- ☐ coloured paper ☐ white paper
- ☐ paper fastener ☐ scissors
- ☐ drawing compasses

The Sun is an average sized star. It is made up of about 75% **hydrogen**, 23% **helium** and 2% metals. Most stars are made up of the same types of **atoms** as our Sun. **Nuclear fusion reactions** take place at the centre of the Sun because here the **temperature**, **pressure** and **density** are very large. In fusion reactions hydrogen is changed to helium and **gamma radiation**. Radiation travels outward from the centre making the surface of the Sun very hot. Heat and light from the surface is radiated into space in all directions. We use some of this energy to live.

At least 4 million tonnes of hydrogen are used up every second on the Sun. It has such a large mass that this will last for about another 5 billion years.

Deuterium + Hydrogen → Helium + gamma ray

Q1 Copy the table.

Elements in a star	%

A Work in a small group. Imagine you have been asked by your local museum to make a short presentation on video about the Sun. The video will be used in the museum to help other students to learn about the Sun. ▼

1 is the **core**. This is where the energy is produced by the nuclear reactions. The temperature is 15 million °C.
2 is the **radiative zone**. Energy travels outward in the form of radiation.
3 is the **convective zone**. Huge convection currents are just below the Sun's surface.
4 is the **photosphere**. This is the shiny bright surface of the Sun. The temperature is about 6000°C.

Never look directly at the Sun. Blindness can result.

Q2 Complete the table.

Q3 What kind of reaction takes place at the centre of the Sun?

Q4 Which gas is used up in this reaction?

Q5 What is produced by this reaction?

Q6 Write down the word and symbol equation for this reaction.

Q7 Why is the Sun's mass decreasing?

Q8 What do you think is happening to its pull of gravity?

Q9 Make a cutout like the planets cutout (page 16) to show information about the four main parts of the Sun.

Extension exercise 8 can be used now.

8 Stars

The life of a star

▶ A large cloud of gas and dust (**nebula**) gathers together over millions of years. The gravity of the gas at the centre pulls the gas inward to form a huge gas ball. The cloud starts to get smaller and **denser**.

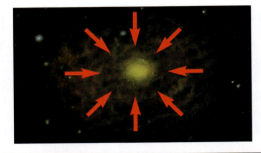

▶ Under the huge pressure the centre starts to break up into smaller bits. The bits are called **protostars** and they vary in size, from one tenth of a **light-year** to one light-year across. The protostars remain together inside the big black cloud in a **cluster**.

Type 1

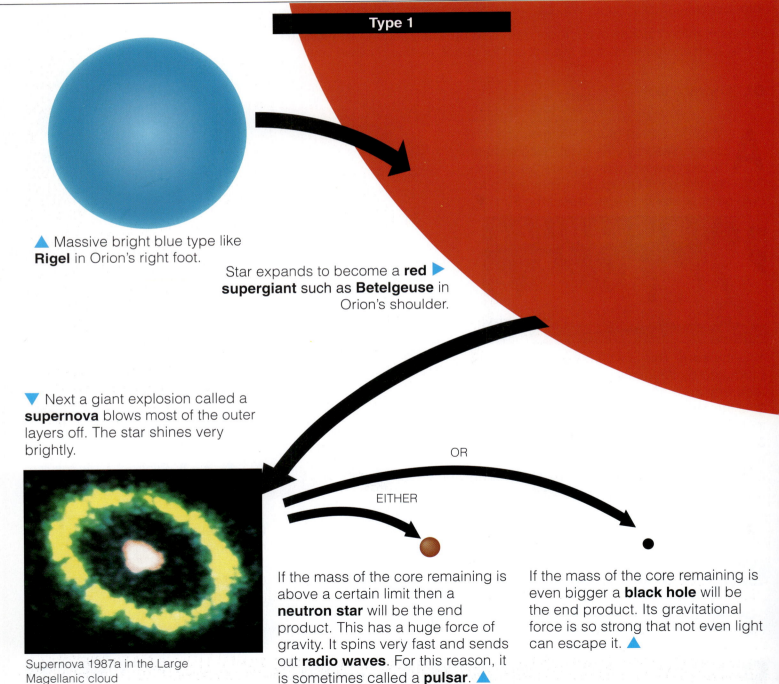

▲ Massive bright blue type like **Rigel** in Orion's right foot.

Star expands to become a **red** ▶
supergiant such as **Betelgeuse** in Orion's shoulder.

▼ Next a giant explosion called a **supernova** blows most of the outer layers off. The star shines very brightly.

Supernova 1987a in the Large Magellanic cloud

EITHER

If the mass of the core remaining is above a certain limit then a **neutron star** will be the end product. This has a huge force of gravity. It spins very fast and sends out **radio waves**. For this reason, it is sometimes called a **pulsar**. ▲

OR

If the mass of the core remaining is even bigger a **black hole** will be the end product. Its gravitational force is so strong that not even light can escape it. ▲

8 Stars

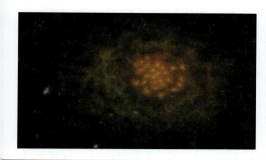

▶ Each protostar looks like a disc with a ball at the centre. The material in the disc could become the star's planets (its solar system). Depending on its mass the protostar can develop into one of two types of star.

Type 2

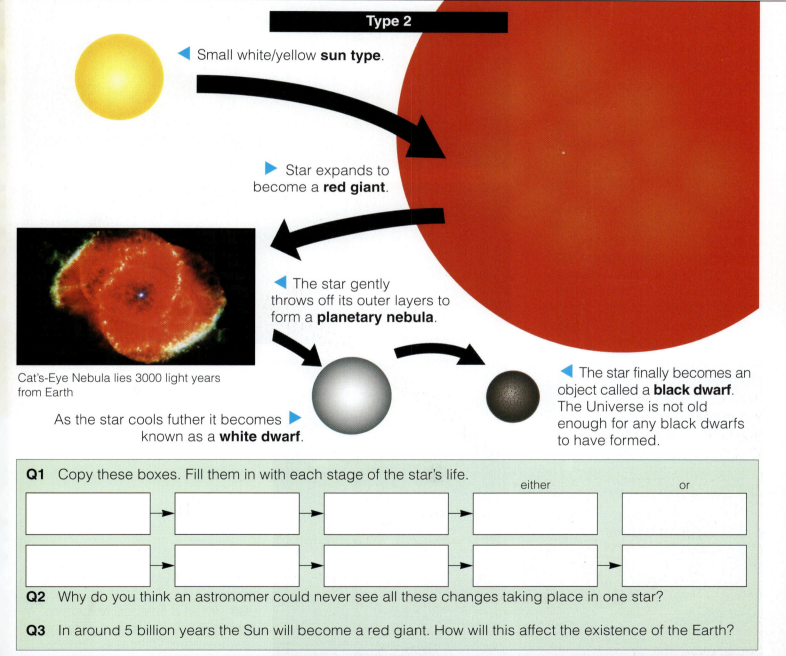

◀ Small white/yellow **sun type**.

▶ Star expands to become a **red giant**.

◀ The star gently throws off its outer layers to form a **planetary nebula**.

Cat's-Eye Nebula lies 3000 light years from Earth

As the star cools futher it becomes ▶ known as a **white dwarf**.

◀ The star finally becomes an object called a **black dwarf**. The Universe is not old enough for any black dwarfs to have formed.

Q1 Copy these boxes. Fill them in with each stage of the star's life.

Q2 Why do you think an astronomer could never see all these changes taking place in one star?

Q3 In around 5 billion years the Sun will become a red giant. How will this affect the existence of the Earth?

Extension exercise 9 can be used now.

9 Galaxies

Apparatus

☐ galaxy handout

Galaxies

Our galaxy is called the Milky Way and our Sun is only one of its 100 billion stars. As well as stars our galaxy contains **nebulae** (dark and bright gas clouds), star clusters, and probably millions of planets too small and dark for us to see. The Milky Way also rotates. Our Solar System is about 25 000 light years from the centre of the galaxy. It takes us 250 million years to travel once around the centre. Parts of the galaxy near the centre complete one revolution in a shorter time than us. Our galaxy is held together by gravity.

▼ The Milky Way is only one of over 20 galaxies in what is called the **Local Group**. The great galaxy in the **constellation** of **Andromeda**, M31 is over 200 000 light years in diameter. It contains about twice as many stars as ours and is about 2.2 million light years away. The Local Group of galaxies is also held together by gravity.

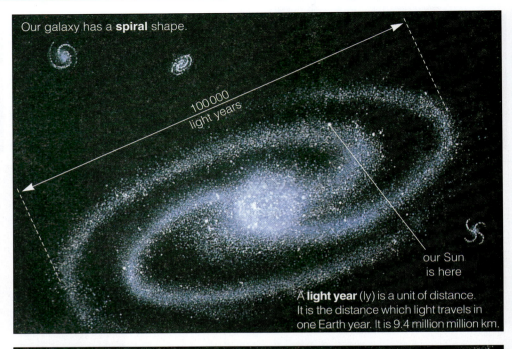

Our galaxy has a **spiral** shape.

100 000 light years

our Sun is here

A **light year** (ly) is a unit of distance. It is the distance which light travels in one Earth year. It is 9.4 million million km.

From the side, the Milky Way looks like a disc.

20 000 light years

position of Sun

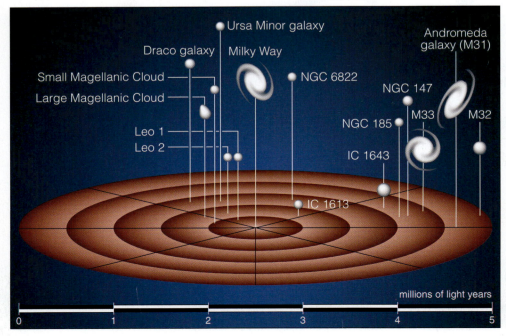

Q1 What is the name of our galaxy?

Q2 How many stars does our galaxy have in it?

Q3 What shape is our galaxy?

Q4 Decribe the position of our Sun in the galaxy.

Q5 Which is the biggest galaxy in the Local Group?

Q6 What difference would you notice if you looked towards the centre of the Milky Way and then looked towards the edge?

9 Galaxies

The expanding Universe

▼ The Universe contains everything that exists, the planets, their moons, the stars, star clusters, the galaxies and groups of galaxies and all the space and gas between them. As far as scientists know there is only one Universe and there is nothing which is not part of it.

Apparatus
- [ ] timescale cutout
- [ ] scissors [ ] glue

There are a hundred thousand million galaxies in the Universe.

The big bang
▲ Most astronomers think that the matter of the Universe was once contained in a hot, **dense** 'fireball'. The fireball exploded about 15 billion years ago. We call this explosion the **'Big Bang'**. All the matter which makes up the Universe (including the matter of our own bodies) came from the big bang.

Through their measurements astronomers believe that the Universe is expanding. For every million light years they are away galaxies increase in speed by around 15 km/s, i.e.:
◄ at 1 million ly → 15 km/s
   at 2 million ly → 30 km/s
   at 3 million ly → 45 km/s

Q1 What is the Universe?

Q2 What is a light year?

Q3 How old is the Universe?

Q4 Where did the galaxies get their energy from to move apart?

Q5 How many galaxies are there in the Universe?

9 Galaxies

Galaxies on the move

Edwin Hubble, an American astronomer found that distant galaxies are moving away from us at great speed. He did this by measuring changes in the **frequency** and **wavelength** of the light from the galaxies. This activity will show similar changes through the use of sound waves in a whistling tube as it moves. Your teacher will set up the sound sensor and data logger.

Apparatus
- plastic whistling-tube
- coloured pencils
- sound sensor   data logger
- computer   printer

⚠ Stand clear of others when you are swinging the tube.

Q1 Copy this table.

Position of tube	Wavelength	Frequency
Moving away		
Moving towards		

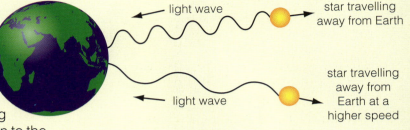

A Work in a small group. Swing a plastic whistling tube quickly above your head. The others listen to the sound and look at the changes on the screen. ▶

As the tube moves away the note is lower in frequency and longer in wavelength. (The wave is stretched.)

As the tube moves towards you the note is higher in frequency and shorter in wavelength. (The wave is squashed.)

This change in frequency and wavelength is called the **Doppler Effect**. Light waves also show this effect.

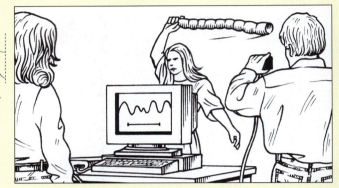

Redshift

We can find out the speed and direction of a star by looking at its **spectrum**. When the light of a star is split up (by a prism in a **spectrometer**) we see dark lines against a background of the seven colours in light. The pattern of the dark lines tells us which elements are in the atmosphere of a star. The position of the pattern, when compared with the bright lines of known **stationary** sources of hydrogen, helium, etc., tells us whether a star is moving with **respect** to Earth.

If a star is moving away the dark lines shift towards the red end of the spectrum. This is called a **redshift**. Red has a longer wavelength than the other colours. It is as though the light wave has been stretched because the star is moving away (just as the sound wave was stretched when the tube was moving away). The faster a star is moving away the greater the redshift.

If a star is not moving away from or towards Earth, the dark lines match up exactly with the position of the bright lines.

Redshift

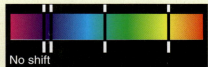
No shift

Extension exercise 10 can be used now.

Q2 Complete the table.

Q3 Mark on your graph where the whistling-tube is moving towards and away.

Q4 Why is the sound of a passing police siren an example of the Doppler Effect?

Q5 What happens to the spectrum of a star which is moving away from us?

Q6 How does the redshift help to explain that we live in an expanding universe?

Q7 Draw and colour a spectrum of a star which is moving away faster than the one shown in the spectrum on the left.

Q8 What do you think would happen to the spectrum of a star which is moving towards us? (Hint: the blue end of the spectrum has shorter wavelengths).